IMAGES
of England

CREWE
THE SECOND SELECTION

The locomotives built in the workshops were proudly driven by a very special set of men who worked over the years in the Crewe North and South Sheds. Enginemen were certainly a tough breed and their job was very demanding on both themselves and their families. It was not unusual for an engineman to say at his retirement presentation, 'My wife should really have this for what she has had to put up with for the past fifty years'. Enginemen had to be prepared to work horrendous shifts, starting and finishing at times when others were either enjoying themselves or asleep. They worked long hours in dirty conditions during rain, fog or snow, often in open cabs. They cooked their meals on the same coal shovel that they used to move tons of coal into the firebox during every shift. While the late Arthur 'Dabber' Davies of Crewe North Sheds was just one of the many thousands of Crewe men who wrestled with the mighty steam engine over the years, his picture really symbolises that special breed of railwaymen who should never be forgotten.

IMAGES
of England

CREWE
THE SECOND SELECTION

Compiled by
Brian Edge

TEMPUS

First published 1999
Copyright © Brian Edge, 1999

Tempus Publishing Limited
The Mill, Brimscombe Port,
Stroud, Gloucestershire, GL5 2QG

ISBN 0 7524 1804 1

Typesetting and origination by
Tempus Publishing Limited
Printed in Great Britain by
Midway Clark Printing, Wiltshire

Few people today will recognize Crewe Green Road as it was in the 1930s. The Crewe Mill, seen on the right, and the rear of the cottages opposite have long since been demolished. The Mill House on the bend in the road now stands alone on an unattractive layby.

Contents

Acknowledgements

Special thanks go to everyone who has helped in any small way with the material for this book. It must be satisfying to know that these valuable records of people and places will be preserved for the benefit of future generations. There is a legal requirement for every published book to be deposited in the British Library, the Libraries of the Universities of Oxford and Cambridge, the National Library of Scotland, the National Library of Wales and the Library of the Trinity College of Dublin. There is, therefore, a pretty good chance that your pictures will be preserved forever.

I would like to thank Mrs Josie Allen, Mrs Audrey Astbury, Mr Derek Baker for coming to my rescue and providing generous help, Kath and Ken Banham, Barry Barker, Philip Barlow, Geoff Bavington, Mrs W.J. Bennett, Mrs Bostock, David Bovington, H. Bullock, The British Railways Board in Derby, Mrs Brown, Miss Kitty Brook, Mrs Maureen Burrows, Brian Butterworth, Miss Joyce Cooper, Mrs E. Davies, Mrs J. Doig, Eardley's *Crewe Almanacks*, Mr and Mrs W.D. Evans, Mrs Beryl Ford, Miss Jean Handbrook, Mr Chris Hardy of Nantwich, Peter Healey, Peter Howard, the late Albert Hunn, Mrs Glenys Huntington, Walter Kirkland, Irene and Bryan Langley, Mr Lupton, Mrs Evelyn Mason, Mr Derrick Mason, Chris Metcalf, John New, Alan Newton, Mrs Hilda Mumford, Peter Ollerhead of Copnal Books in Meredith Street, Crewe, for his valuable assistance, Bernard and Joy Owen for their help and for their dedicated contribution to local history, Gladys and John Percival of Sound, Mrs Elsie Perkins (a true Sydneyite), H.B. Pie, Mrs Daisy Proudman, the late Mrs Em. Roddan, Margaret Sharpes, Mrs D.H. Teasdale, Joe Thorley, Mrs Louie Turner, Mr R. Passey, Anthony Phillips, Peter F. Walker, John Wolstenholme, Christine Wood, Colin Wood and Frank Wright.

Many of the Haslington pictures were taken by the late Walter Birchenough, a professional photographer who lived at 2 Wellesley Avenue, Haslington, until his death around 1960. A very special thank you must go to Jean and Norman Walsh of Wistaston for the loan of these splendid photographs. I would also like to especially thank Mick and Beryl Warwick for so generously allowing me to hunt through their family albums and to reproduce numerous photographs. I have tried very hard not to forget anyone who has helped in any way, however small, but should I have forgotten anyone then please put it down to human error and accept these sincere thanks. Finally, I have had to rely entirely on others to provide names of individuals featured on the photographs. Apologies are therefore offered to those who have not been identified, those who may have been wrongly identified and for any misspellings of names.

Brian Edge
May 1999

Introduction

Little is left today to remind us that Crewe was once one of the world's most famous centres of railway activity. Much of the town of Crewe was built and owned by the railway including its houses, schools, places of worship, swimming baths, library, hospital and its gas, water and electricity supply. During the great age of steam the inhabitants relied entirely on the railway industry for their livelihood. This book contains photographs of railways, street scenes, buildings, events concerning Crewe and its people as well as a look at Wistaston and Haslington in days gone by.

A special feature of the town in the late nineteenth century was the unique Crewe Works' Army, the 2nd Cheshire Royal Engineers (Railway Volunteers). The people of Crewe were justifiably proud of these men who distinguished themselves in the Boer War in South Africa from 1899 to 1902. A few more archive photographs are included to complement those in the first book from this series, which included a history of the reservists. Fred Walker, a Crewe man who worked in the machine shop of the Old Crewe Railway Works, was a reservist with the Warwickshire Regiment. When he was recalled to his regiment, his shop mates made him a gift labelled, 'He's a gentleman in Kharki (sic) ordered South – November 17th 1899', thus demonstrating the affection and esteem that Crewe folk had for their colleagues and townsfolk. This feeling is supported by the crowds who lined the streets when their men marched off to war.

It is not just buildings that have changed over the years, lifestyles have changed too. Sixty years ago the Crewe park was packed at weekends. Townsfolk turned up to take part in a sporting activity, listen to the band, have a sail on the lake, walk around, meet and chat with friends or generally soak up the beauty of the place. While lifestyles have changed, Queen's Park remains a very beautiful place. An inscription on one of the seats reads 'in memory of the happy days we spent in Queen's Park'.

As a girl Mrs Evelyn Mason (now aged ninety) lived at 41 Stewart Street and went to the Stewart Street School, which has now become a private residence. Mrs Mason recalls going to Collins' the grocers on the corner of Alton Street and Stewart Street to get a canvas sugar bag for pegging a rug during the dark nights. The rugs were made of old coats and it was useful if you could find an old red coat as this colour would go in the middle of the design to brighten up the finished rug. Mrs Mason's father made the wooden peg to enable her to push the cloth through the canvas. At night her family would stand around the piano and sing. On Friday nights (wages day) in the 1920s she would go to the Congregational church on Hightown to pay the 'Congo'. This was a Christmas club where you paid what you could afford and had a pay-out at Christmas. As Mrs Mason recalls, 'hundreds upon hundreds would turn up to pay, everybody seemed to do it.'

Living near to the gasworks, Mrs Mason recalls that mothers would regularly bring their children who suffered from bronchial complaints to breathe in the air! When her mother needed a gas mantle, she would go to the offices at the gasworks to buy one. Around 1919 she recalls going 'Souling' on All Souls night. The boys and girls would chant, 'Soul, soul an apple or two, if you haven't got an apple a pear will do, if you haven't got a pear a halfpenny will do, and if you haven't got a halfpenny God bless you.'

On Wednesday 28 May 1919 the Wistaston Estate was put up for auction by the owner Brigadier-General Walthall, DSO (see p. 118). Henry Manley conducted the sale which was held in the Royal Hotel. The offering was described as 'Wistaston Hall, a well-known country mansion with picturesque park-like surroundings, an absolutely Free fully licensed public house with twenty-one acres of pasture land known as the "Rising Sun", eight well-known farms and ten smallholdings. Eleven dwelling houses and cottages, an attractive bungalow, a characteristic villa residence, a valuable sand pit, a field and fox covert and many valuable lots of land ripe for development into building sites. The estate agent was Mr John Loring of Doddington, Nantwich.' The farms offered for sale were: White House Farm on Valley Road, occupied by George Evanson; Moat House Farm on Valley Road, occupied by F. Woodcock; The Rockwood Farm off Alton Street, occupied by F. Woodcock; Wistaston Green Farm off Wistaston Green Road, occupied by Mr George Reade; Old Gorse Farm at Wistaston Green, occupied by Mr W.H. Merrill; West End Farm at Wistaston Green, occupied by George Siddall; Robinsons Corner Farm, approached by a short road off the Nantwich to Middlewich Road, occupied by T.H. Wilkinson; Church House Farm, Wistaston, occupied by G.H. Crewe; Whitegates Farm, a smallholding on Wistaston Green Road, occupied by G. Holland; and Wells Green Farm, occupied by E. Smith. The field and covert near Wistaston Hall (now the recreational field), an area of around seventeen acres including a considerable quantity of valuable growing timber in the wood and on the land, sold for £960. Messrs Greenhall Whitley bought the Rising Sun Inn for £3,800.

From that day on Wistaston began to urbanise until most traces of this delightful piece of rural Cheshire disappeared forever. It was a blessing that, in the 1970s, the Wistaston Parish Council resisted the attempts of a Birmingham based developer to buy the field and covert mentioned above for a housing estate. Whitegates Farm (see above) is recalled in the Wistaston section of this book.

Most readers will agree that we cannot live in the past, we must move on. Crewe is no different from any other town, all have had to make drastic changes, but it is nice to secretly believe that there was nothing like the good old days and perhaps this book will help you to recall some of them.

Brian Edge
May 1999

One
Railways and Other Transport

The South African Memorial in Queen's Park was erected as a tribute to the 2nd Cheshire Royal Engineers (Railway Volunteers) who served with distinction in the Boer War. The statue made of labradorite and grey Aberdeen granite was unveiled on 8 August 1903 by Lord Stalbridge, chairman of the board of the London and North Western Railway. At the base of the column, for many years, was a bronze coloured model engine No. 1942, *Edward VII*, which was made by Mr Harry Lightfoot of Buxton Avenue, a locomotive works fitter. For security reasons it was removed from its position on the memorial a number of years ago, but it can now be seen in the reception area of the Municipal Buildings.

Five young members of the Crewe Works Army, otherwise known as the 2nd Cheshire Royal Engineers. This is a fine record of their smart uniforms which had nine white metal buttons bearing the monogram VR (Victoria Regina) with a crowned garter around, on which were the words 'Volunteer Engineers'. The Royal Engineers wore a series of different hats over the years from the pillbox type to policemen's helmets and, in this case, the forage cap. The collar dogs feature Crewe locomotive No. 3000 facing inwards. The townsfolk were rightly proud of the Crewe Works Army.

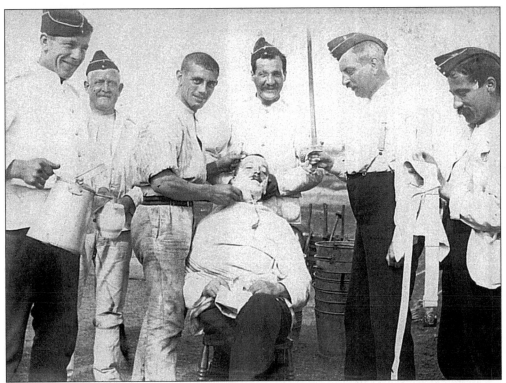

The Drum Major prepares to shave Quartermaster Sergeant Gibson with a ceremonial sword while at camp at Rhyl in 1895.

Collection of rations, 6.45 a.m., at Rhyl in July 1895.

Pitching tents at Rhyl in July 1895.

The Volunteer Engineers at their rifle range under the Holmes Chapel railway viaduct in August 1895.

H. Stafford playing his home-made cigar box violin to the Reservists' mascot, Major, while on exercise at Rhyl in July 1895.

An advance party of Railway Volunteer Engineers assembled on Crewe Square in 1902. During this period the men wore policeman-style helmets. The men, who are on their way to Aldershot, stand near where the war memorial stands today. Coppenhall Terrace (now Queensway) is behind the lamp-post and the buildings to the right are now the site of Marks and Spencer. The tall gabled building on the right is the Central School of Music, a piano and organ warehouse.

The 2nd Cheshire Volunteer Engineers marching off to war on 16 October 1899. The 6 companies, each of 100 men, were made up of engine drivers, firemen, cleaners, fitters, boilermakers, riveters, smiths, platelayers, shunters and pointsmen. The men are marching down High Street, while Eaton Street and the Deviation Gate can be seen in the distance. The area where the Ming Sum Chinese restaurant is now can be seen on the right. The notices on the left advertise a new jeweller, C.H. Moody, who is still in business today. Note a man in the crowd hugging his friend, the man up the lamp-post and those waving flags on the roof.

The 10th Company of the 2nd Cheshire Royal Engineers upon arrival at Cape Town in 1899.

Quartermaster Sergeant Gibson caught by a brave photographer while having a crafty nap at Chatham in July 1900. It is on record that Gibson presided over a Smoking Concert which was held in the Old Vaults Hotel, Earle Street, on 25 September 1902. The gathering consisted of Volunteer Engineers who had taken part in the South African campaign.

Workers in the forge at Crewe Works, c. 1906. The man on the left of the back row is Jimmy Moore. From the left, the first three on the front row are: Sammy Ainsworth, Mr Cope, Charles Morris. The others are unknown. Charles Morris (1876-1923) lived at 41 Stewart Street. The picture shows his waistcoat covered with spark burns: the larger burns have been patched. Charles had the first week in July off for holiday each year but did not get paid for it.

This Crewe-built locomotive is working on the Malines–Terneuzen railway in Belgium, *c.* 1905. It is a former London and North Western DX goods locomotive and was built sometime between 1858 and 1874. It is interesting to note that it still carries its old Crewe number plate, 3115.

Another similar type of Crewe-built locomotive working on the same Belgian railway. This engine was rebuilt since its Crewe days.

Columbine, one of the early Crewe-built locomotives, is seen here with the purpose-built Chief Mechanical Engineer's Inspection Coupe – a delightful creation. The Coupe was kept alongside the Steam Fire Engine, under one of the arches of Chester Bridge.

Trevithic's *Cornwall* was built in 1847 and had 8ft 6in driving wheels. It originally had an underslung boiler to give a lower centre of gravity but this was unsatisfactory. In 1858 it was rebuilt to F.W. Webb's drawings with the boiler above the driving axle. It was rumoured to have attained 117mph down Madeley Bank! Originally numbered 173, it was given number 3020 in 1886. The next year it was given a new boiler and a circular smoke box door. *Cornwall* worked on fast Liverpool to Manchester expresses from 1890 until 1902, but was withdrawn from service in December 1907. The engine was restored to service in 1911 and was attached to the Chief Mechanical Engineer's Saloon. It later worked as a service locomotive again until after 1923 and is now a preserved locomotive.

Shades of a great past. A pre-war view of Crewe North Sheds where a gleaming Royal Scot Class No. 6106, *Gordon Highlander*, stands in the centre of the picture with Patriot Class No. 5529 to the right and a Jubilee Class locomotive on the extreme right.

Inside Crewe North Sheds during the same period. Stanier *Black 5*, No. 5373, occupies the centre road with a Royal Scot Class engine to the left.

Crewe Works in the days of London, Midland and Scottish Railway. Royal Scot Class Locomotive No. 6121 is being lifted from the track. The engine was built in 1928 and named *H.L.I.* It was rebuilt in 1946, along with others in its class, and renumbered 46121 in October 1948. In 1949 it was renamed *Highland Light Infantry, City of Glasgow Regiment*, but was withdrawn from service and scrapped in 1962.

The Eagle Bridge within Crewe Locomotive Works in 1971. The fine eagles shown here can now be seen at the works' entrances on West Street and Victoria Avenue and two are located at 'The Railway Age (Crewe Heritage Centre).

Deep in the Second World War and deep in snow. A bleak and deserted view of Crewe North Junction in January 1940. The old Crewe North box can be seen behind the new box which, along with its partner at Crewe South, was built in the style of an air raid shelter to withstand enemy bombing.

A lone engine braves the storm at Crewe North Junction in January 1940.

The north end of Crewe station in the snow of January 1940. A northbound express stands at the main platform. The Crewe Arms Hotel can be seen on the left of the picture. The abandoned handcart and the lone worker add a little warmth to this uninviting scene.

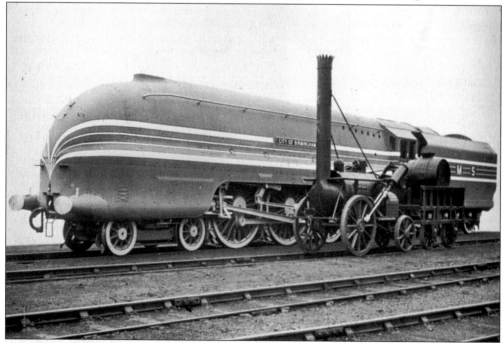

Crewe-built Princess Coronation Class locomotive No. 6235, *City of Birmingham*, is shown here alongside a replica of the *Rocket*. People looking at the locomotive around the time the picture was taken, would be justified in thinking that nothing could ever be produced to better this design.

Officials with bowler hats examine Princess Coronation Class locomotive No. 6220, *Coronation*, at Crewe station on 28 May 1937, just a fortnight after the Coronation of King George VI and Queen Elizabeth. Four weeks later on Tuesday 29 June 1937, this engine achieved a record speed of 114mph between Whitmore and Crewe. Tom Clark, the Crewe driver on this occasion, was also a Royal Train driver. He was personally awarded the OBE by King George VI after one of his Royal Train journeys.

There was no better experience for a trainspotter on the west coast main line in pre-war years than the sight of a Coronation Class, nicknamed 'Streak', clattering by at high speed.

A group of railway veterans assembled outside the LMS General Offices, c. 1940. They are in front of Princess Coronation Class No. 6245, *City of London*, which was built in Crewe. The veterans, many born in Crewe in the 1850s, proudly wear their lapel badges. Committee members wore white badges and ordinary members blue. The London and North Western Railway Veterans' Institute (later the Railway Veterans' Institute) was founded in 1917. The occasion of this gathering is unknown. Second from the right is William Cooper, a foreman bricklayer for the London and North Western Railway Company, who lived at Wrinehill. One of the jobs that he and his men had to carry out was the building of Edge Hill Sheds. To get to work each week William had to walk about seven miles from Wrinehill to the station to get his train to Liverpool and he had to walk back again at the end of the week. His mother packed him up as much food as possible to last him the week and he would carry this with him on his trek to the station. During this period roads were very lonely and there were problems with footpads. To combat any possible trouble while walking to work, William always carried a blunderbuss with him! One of William's jobs on the committee of the 'old vets' was to purchase tea in bulk and to sell packets of the commodity to other members at the lowest possible price: a sure sign that some of the retired members suffered considerable hardship.

At one period in the Second World War, the railways of Britain had nearly 20,000 staff in 35 of their workshops engaged in the production of armaments. The work included tanks, aircraft, guns, shells, bombs, tools, midget submarine superstructures, landing craft and Bailey bridges. Tanks and aircraft, however, constituted the main part of the work done. The first call came in July 1937, over two years before the inevitable war was declared. The War Office asked the London, Midland and Scottish Railway to carry out the design of a medium tank. A pilot model known as the A14 was subsequently built at Crewe Works but before it was finished the War Office decided that a lighter and less costly vehicle was needed. Accordingly, the LMS undertook the design of a new machine which was eventually christened the Covenanter. The LMS built 1,771 Covenanters, with Crewe Works building 161 of them and additionally repairing and modifying 150 of the total number, in accordance with War Office requirements.

The General Offices on Chester Bridge in 1945. Union flags abound and victory is being celebrated.

'We've a bit of a problem at Crewe North!' Note the private owners' wagons, a feature of pre-nationalisation railways.

'Oh dear! The LMS are in an 'ell of a mess!' Crewe North signal box, which can be seen in the background, was built in 1940 in the style of an air raid shelter to withstand enemy attack.

A bowler-hatted official to subordinate, 'I shall want a report in quadruplicate about this!'

The LMS van was soon back on its wheels and the bogie bolster and its cargo of steel plates on its way. The steam crane, outrigged and secured down, can be seen at work.

Miss Hilda Cooper was the Crewe Locomotive Queen in 1938-39. Apart from featuring in the Crewe Hospital Fête, which is now known as the Crewe Carnival, Hilda (now Mrs Mumford) carried out many other duties during her reign as Locomotive Queen. One particularly memorable event was a tour of Crewe Works where she was enthusiastically welcomed by all the workmen. One of the attractions of the fête in 1939 was the seemingly obsolete sport of 'push ball' which involved the pushing of a ball that was about eight feet in height. At the time, this sport was sponsored by the *Daily Mail* but there seems to be little known about it today.

Miss Hilda Cooper being greeted in the Municipal Buildings by the Mayor Councillor Kelsall and his wife along with Mr Hugh and the Mayor's attendant.

The Crewe Steam Shed Band was established in 1868.

This was how people travelled around the town 100 years ago. This splendid horse-drawn bus advertises, 'Macdonald's Teeth – Painless System'. The indicator board shows that this bus ran from Hungerford Road to the station. Note the conductor on the left wearing his official badge and complete with his cash bag. It seems that the horses were also contracted to the local fire brigade as, when the fire bell sounded, it was not unusual for the driver to unhitch the horses and gallop them off to the fire station, leaving the passengers to walk!

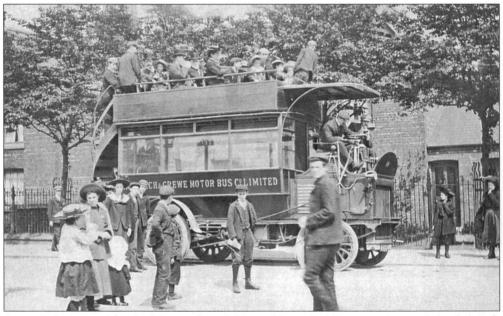

An early bus owned by the Nantwich and Crewe Motor Bus Company Limited, loaded with passengers. The bus, registration number M 878, had solid tyres and was restricted to 12mph.

Crosville single-decker No. 250, which was used on the Crewe to Audley route, around 1922. The driver, John Mason (left), worked for Crosville Crewe from 1920 to 1960 and ended his service as Crewe Depot Manager. While working as a driver, John was summoned for driving at an estimated speed of 18mph along Calveley Straight. He appeared at Oakmere Petty Sessions and was fined as the bus had a restricted speed of 12mph. The conductor, or guard as they were sometimes known, was Wilf Dodd and he is wearing a typical example of a conductor's uniform. Note the leather cuffs on his sleeves to prevent chafing on his ticket machine and cash bag. It is almost possible to hear one of the familiar refrains: 'Move right down the bus please!', 'Only eight standing!', 'Plenty of room on top!', 'Hold tight please!', 'Sorry, full bus!'

Crewe's first bus station was opened on 21 June 1960 by the Mayor of Crewe, Councillor S. Orwell JP. The site on which the bus station now stands was originally used for dwelling houses occupied by railway employees. The site was purchased by the Omnibus Company from the Crewe Corporation and the work was started in April 1959. Prior to the station being built, buses ran from three points: Crewe Square, Prince Albert Street and Chester Street. Passengers changing services had to walk 350 yards. The provision of a bus station avoided this as passengers could then change services completely under cover.

A Crosville 'Bristol' (Low Bridge) double-decker, route number 203, bound for Willaston Station via Valley Road, leaves Crewe Square in the late 1950s. Passengers can be seen waiting for the arrival of their buses. Barclays Bank is on the left and the old District Bank (now the National Westminster Bank) is on the right.

Another Crosville 'Bristol' double-decker in Delamere Street in 1959. The indicator blind reads Beech Drive.

Mr Venables, a carter, with his horse in the Corporation Yard. The yard was off Market Street at the cemetery end. Mr Venables looked after two horses which were stabled in the yard during winter and kept in a field during the summer. They were shod at Simpsons in South Street. Mr Venables often obtained a concoction of boiled up linseed, meal and black treacle from Mr Mavor to give to the horses when they were unwell. There was a tar boiler in the yard and when local children had a cold they were given a bit of tarred rope to inhale.

A view of the Corporation Yard showing a group of workers. The building in the background is the joiner's shop. The man in a cap second left was Mr Malt.

The late Mr Les Wood of 14 Frank Webb Avenue, Crewe, used to drive this Ford loudspeaker van for Vernon Cooper the electrical, radio and early television engineers. The van could be seen at events such as fêtes and carnivals.

Two
Buildings and Street Scenes

Crewe Street was demolished in the early 1960s. The identity and present whereabouts of the mother and children are unknown.

Pioneer Angling and Social Club, Oak Street, in the mid-1950s. The club had a strict rule that no ladies were allowed in the bar. There was, however, a special room for ladies and they had their own waiter. The club had nearly 2,000 social members but only a few hundred angling members, though the latter were the only ones to vote on an issue. There were no female angling members. The motor car in the picture is a Hillman Minx and readers will see by the sign on the left that Oak Street was, at this time, a one-way road.

Bill Nield, the steward of the Pioneer Angling and Social Club, and his wife Clara outside the main entrance. Bill became the steward in 1952. When the club was demolished around 1960, a new club was built in Underwood Lane. Bill and Clara continued to work there until around 1967.

Demolition of part of the Pioneer Angling and Social Club is now complete. There is a good view of Exchange Street shops on the left. The Oak Street sign can be seen on the side of the club. The Crosville Bus K25 is on its way to Valley Road. The van belongs to Singleton & Cole Ltd, wholesale tobacconists and confectioners. The lady appears to be having trouble with her NSU 'Quickly' moped.

The beginning of the demolition of the Pioneer Angling and Social Club in the early 1960s. Breeden House now occupies the site. Note the small shops in Exchange Street, now Market Street.

Exchange Street, now Market Street, in 1940. This view was taken from outside the Christadelphian church. The buildings opposite, long since demolished, made way for Breeden House. It is interesting to note that the two shops opposite seem to have been added outside the building line. The signpost indicates the way to the nearest public air raid shelter. The building by the Belisha Beacon is the Pioneer Angling and Social Club. The street lighting consisted of single lamps suspended by wires centrally over the middle of the road, although it is doubtful that they were in use at the time the picture was taken as there was a blackout.

The North Shed Enginemen's Barracks were built in 1867 to accommodate men between shifts and had around forty beds. The barracks was in use until around 1970, but was demolished in the mid-1970s. The registration number of the vehicle in the picture is 7650 VT. The London and North Western Railway Hospital, which stood in the old works at the bottom of Oak Street, can be seen above the bridge.

Old Crewe Town. Prince Albert Street and the corner of Liverpool Street in 1961. Christ Church can be seen in the distance. The site is now occupied by the Crewe public library.

Moore and Brock's shop on the corner of Earle Street and Prince Albert Street, c. 1969. To the right is the entrance to the Town Hall and the Library (Mechanics' Institute). The shop was once the Euston Coffee Tavern, opened in 1880 by Francis W. Webb. The tavern offered moderately priced refreshments and was open for morning coffee from 5.30 a.m. onwards! The building had a commercial room which could be hired out for events such as social gatherings and property sales. The tavern was also a LNWR depot where parcels could be taken for dispatch by rail. It was managed by a sub-committee of the Cottage Hospital Management Committee and all profits from the enterprise were devoted to the Crewe Cottage Hospital. The secretary in 1912 was Mr F. Chesworth of 17 Gainsborough Road. The buildings were demolished in the early 1970s and the present law courts, police station and public library erected.

The following seven pictures tell the story of the life and demise of a popular Crewe shop. This is E. Barnett's tobacconist shop at 85 Mill Street in 1912 when it had been especially decorated with bunting and coloured electric lights for the visit of King George V and Queen Mary. The newspaper adverts of the *Daily Dispatch* and the *Daily News* announced the royal visit. Other newspapers seen advertised in this picture are the *Sportsman Daily*, which cost one penny, and *Lloyds News*, 'the most popular newspaper in the world'. Mr E. Barnett is seen standing in the doorway.

Looking down Union Street from Barnett's in 1939. Sunblinds were a feature of most shops around this time. It was often possible to see shop assistants with a short pole adjusting the position of the blinds according to the weather. The blinds protected the stock on display and also allowed shelter for the prospective customer. Note the old style, Halt at Major Road Ahead sign, and Edleston Road School in the distance.

John Barnett's wholesale and retail tobacconist's shop in the 1930s which, at the time, incorporated a ladies' and gentlemen's hairdresser. Mr John Barnett, the son of E. Barnett, and his staff stand proudly outside the shop with its fascinating window display. The shop sold Players' Country Life cigarettes and tobacco, as well as Players' Navy Cut Medium cigarettes. There is an array of pipes on show and the thermometer on the left of the window advertises Stephens Inks. Cigars cost 5d and 8d each and the ladies' hairdresser provided the latest Eugene Permanent Wave for just 21 shillings.

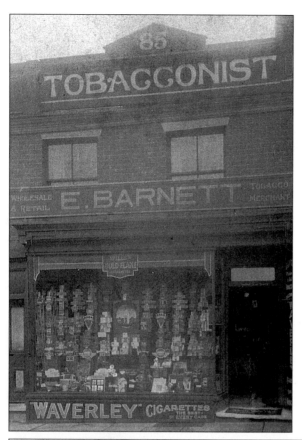

E. Barnett's shop, emblazoned with TOBACCONIST, advertises Waverley cigarettes ('the best in every case!'), while the rubber doormat advertises Swan Vestas matches.

This gives a better idea of the setting of Barnett's shop in Mill Street. The sunblind reads, established 1886. The shop next door is described as a 'High Class Chocolate and Sweet Store, Novelties, Confectionery, Minerals and Ices'. It was clearly a hot day as the blind against the window was necessary to protect the window display from the sun.

A sad day as the popular shop faces demolition in 1969. It served the public for eighty-three years.

The rear of 85 Mill Street at the time of demolition in 1969.

The Albion Hotel in Mill Street contributed a superb window decoration for the visit of King George V and Queen Mary on 21 April 1913.

Webster's of Crewe in 1969. This shop was on the corner of Station Street and Mill Street, on the opposite side of the road to where it stands today. The shop front advertises Trojan, Isetta and Reliant cars.

Looking down Railway Street towards Pedley Street. Thousands of enginemen would walk up and down Railway Street to and from their work in the North Sheds. No doubt the corner shop which sold Park Drive cigarettes from a vending machine had a little gold mine on its hands.

Looking down Station Street in the late 1960s. The location of the once famous Crewe North Engine Sheds can be seen on the left, just beyond the Queen's Hotel, an Ind Coope house. The Austin A40 bears the registration number JEY 795. The vehicle parked behind is a Morris Traveller.

The Railway Hotel, *c.* 1968. This scene looks down Station Street towards Mill Street, where Webster's shop can be seen. The Railway public house on the corner of Wesley Street specialised in Walker's Ales.

Looking down Mill Street from Nantwich Road, prior to the road-widening scheme in the 1980s. Eric Preston ran a chemist's which was also the Nantwich Road post office. The sign above the main door reads, National Health Insurance Dispensary. The large poster advertises Thwaites Ales. The shops on the left of Mill Street included a solicitor, a cabinetmaker, a poodle parlour and Derek Baker's Stamp and Collectors shop.

A similar view showing the shops on Nantwich Road. The shop to the left of the traffic lights was Custom Amplification, which now operates in Edleston Road. It was always guarded by a large Alsation. The next shop to the left was Mrs Bright's chemist. Most of the shops had compulsory purchase orders placed on them for the purpose of widening Mill Street around 1981. The shops mostly remained derelict for a few years before the work was eventually completed.

A last look at Harper's Ironmongers on the corner of Nantwich Road and South Street. The shop was run for a number of years by Cyril Alcock and his wife. The Barrel public house can be seen on the left. The small shop in between was Bill Tyrer's florist.

A much earlier view of the Nantwich Road block of shops from the previous page, showing the changes a few years can make. The familiar figure in a white overall emerging from Bright's is the late Elwin New. Elwin started work as manager for Mrs Bright in 1947 and when Mrs Bright died, around 1959, Elwin and his wife Nancy became the proprietors, remaining in business there until 30 December 1982. Elwin will be remembered by many Crewe people who were patrons of his delightful old-style chemist's shop. His stock was displayed all around the shop in glass cases and on top of these were bottles of coloured liquids, which symbolised the trade. The counter was stacked high with cabinets and there was a small aperture, about five feet square, which Elwin or Nancy would quietly and almost mysteriously appear from when a customer entered the shop. The balconies over the shops were the dress circle for watching the annual carnival pass by. Other shops shown are Lena Blume's wool, knitting, sewing and haberdashers, Broxton's butchers, Hough's newsagents and Maureen's ladies hairdressers.

The Earl of Crewe Hotel in the 1920s. The hotel proprietor at this time was Harry Bricker and later his son Gerald became the licensee. The hotel sold petrol, oil, tyres and provided a full repair service in their garage. The hotel offered a fine bowling green with a large pavilion and billiards. It was a fine building, although today it lacks the central tower which made the building so attractive. The petrol pumps can be seen on the right. The hotel's jingle was:

'Twixt you and me, that's me and you,
Lost! Where to go and what to do,
You're always made welcome, no matter how few,
When you give us a call at the Earl of Crewe!'

A roadman works in Smallman Road almost 100 years ago. The picture shows the very attractive terrace of bay-fronted houses which seem so different when the street is full of parked cars.

This view of the Ursuline Convent in Nantwich Road was taken by E. Lyon who lived at Station Bridge, Crewe. The building is now the Cheshire Constabulary Training Centre and Maintenance headquarters.

The dining room at the Ursuline Convent, c. 1910.

Ruskin Road around 1910. There is a remarkable difference today as the trees in front of the school are fully grown and the entire road is lined on both sides with trees.

Valley Brook in 1923. The houses on the left are in Alton Street and those facing are the backs of buildings in Flag Lane. The new Flag Lane Bridge can be seen between the two blocks of houses.

Crowds gather on a dull and chilly 7 November 1923 for the official opening of Flag Lane Bridge. Note the bare site where the Crewe swimming baths stand today. The two buses were provided by Gibson's Garage of Crewe. The ceremony was carried out by the Mayoress of Crewe Mrs J.R. Goulden.

Barnfield Cottages in Hightown were built in 1854 and demolished in 1969 to create yet another car park.

A view of 6 Heathfield Avenue, Crewe, a century ago. The building survives today although the transformation is perhaps disappointing.

St Paul's Church, Hightown, around 100 years ago. The building is now used as a store for old furniture by a charitable organization. Beyond the church the block of houses in Albert Street has long since been demolished.

Crewe town square on 29 April 1918. The Mayor Mr J.H. Kettell and other dignitaries stand on an early tank (Tin Lizzie No. 137, named *Drake*) appealing to the crowd to buy War Savings Bonds and Certificates. The jingle used was 'Bank at the tank'. Market Street can be seen on the right and the site of the facing Unemployment Exchange is today the side of Marks and Spencer. Off picture are further crowds of people and a large platform festooned with bunting on which Foden's Band performed.

The Blue Cap Dog, an old Tetley's pub on Market Street. Heath Street is on the left of the picture.

New shops were built in Victoria Street between 1957 and 1958. The shop on the corner is now the Abbey National building society.

The old Empire Cinema in Heath Street finished its life as a bingo hall.

The corner of Earle Street and Cobden Street before demolition took place for the new road. The building on the corner was originally a small pub named the Old Vaults and nicknamed the Pig and Whistle.

56

A final look at Market Street prior to demolition. The old Grand Junction Hotel can be seen on the left.

Co-operative Street just prior to demolition. The Ritz Cinema can be seen at the end of the street on the right. Its predecessor was known as The Kino and it was still referred to by this name, even after it became the Ritz.

A very early photograph of Elk's Bakery in Farrington Street, which was located at the bottom end of John Street, off Albert Street. Bags of flour and freshly baked loaves can be seen inside the building. The young boy on the right seen holding a basket of loaves is Frank Kettle who became an officer in the West Street Baptist Boys Life Brigade around 1908 (see p. 75).

The Samuel Heath Memorial Church in Ramsbottom Street in the late 1960s, just before it was demolished. Samuel Heath built the chapel, the portico of which was originally part of the old Macclesfield railway station. It is said that Heath built Ramsbottom Street wider than some of the other streets he built so that the viewer could obtain a better perspective of this impressive frontage.

A charming old cottage which once stood at the corner of Waldrens Lane and Stoneley Road. It was the home of Mrs Emmett who can be seen on the left. The building was demolished many years ago.

Robert Offley Ashburton Crewe-Milnes, the Earl of Crewe, c. 1897.

The Technical Schools were opened by the Earl of Crewe on 16 October 1897. At present this fine building, like so many of its kind throughout the country, is unused and derelict. This picture was taken before all of the windows had originally been put in. Castle Street, which can be seen on the left, was demolished around thirty years ago.

The Crewe Isolation Diseases Hospital was opened by the Earl of Crewe on the same day as the Technical Schools. The buildings were demolished in the late 1970s to make way for a modern housing estate.

The Christian Brethren's meeting room in Glover Street at the time of its opening, *c.* 1931. The meetings listed on the board outside are: Lord's Day – Breaking of Bread at 11 a.m., Sunday school at 2.15, Bible reading at 3.15, Gospel Meeting at 6.30; Prayer Meeting at 7.30 on Monday; Bible reading at 7.30 on Wednesday. The preacher at the opening ceremony was J. Seddon of Sutton whose name is chalked in the space provided on the board. Local children wrote up the name of a certain Count Bartelli as preacher on several occasions. The building still exists and has been extended, but the boundary wall in front has disappeared. The photograph was taken by Walton's Studio, 109 Mill Street, Crewe.

The Brooklands, Crewe, almost 100 years ago.

The last days of the old three-storey Fustian Factory in Walker Street, which was built in 1871 by Thomas Sheppard. The factory was known as the Alexandria Mill and employed around 130 women full time. Fustian was a coarse cotton material with a pile like velvet. The factory was under the control of the United Velvet Cutter's Association and was active until the late 1920s. The building became an ironworks and was finally demolished in the 1960s.

Wheelman Road, Tottys Hall Estate, in November 1969. The buildings were demolished prior to the building of Leighton Park.

The Coach and Horses Inn, Bradfield Green. A charming scene from before the days of breathalysers and crash helmets. The Austin's number plate reads BMB 41 and the motorcycle's 332 GMB. These are both Chester registrations. The inn's sign indicates that it is a Greenhall Whitley House.

The Coach and Horses Inn, Bradfield Green, in the 1930s.

Members of a fishing trip pose outside the Coach and Horses Inn, *c.* 1920.

Crewe Park, around 100 years ago, showing the L.N.W.R. pavilion and bandstand. The bandstand was relocated, allowing the South African War Memorial to be erected in 1903.

Crewe Park in the early 1900s. The picture says something for global warming!

Three

Nineteenth-Century
Advertising

James B. Price, coach proprietor. In modern everyday life landaus, waggonettes, broughams and carriages have all disappeared. Note the telephone number is 22, which is considerably shorter than today's! This advertisement and the following ones in this section are all 100 years old.

List of a few very special Bargains in
Good, Reliable Second-hand
Pianos, Organs, &c.
Now being offered by
J. BENTLEY.

				£	s.	d.
Good Second-hand Piano, in fine condition, good tone, by *Broadwood*				5	0	0
Good Modern do.	do.	do. by *Hopkinson*		6	0	0
Good do.	do.	do. by *Dreaper*		7	0	0
Superior do.	do.	do. by *Lange*		8	0	0
Do. do.	do.	do. by *Chappell*		10	0	0
Do. do,	do.	do. by *Rintoul*		10	10	0
Very Good do.	do.	do. by *Rintoul*		12	0	0
Do. do.	do.	do. by *Oetzman*		14	0	0
Do. do.	do.	do. by *Hopkinson*		15	0	0
Splendid iron-framed do. trichord, check action, every improvement, nearly new				16	0	0
Splendid do., nearly new, by *Bord*				15	0	0
Superb do., with every improvement, nearly new, by *John Brinsmead & Sons* (a rare bargain)..				23	0	0
American Organ, knee swell, fine tone				5	0	0
Do. do.	do.	4 stops..		6	0	0
Do. do.	do.	7 stops..		8	0	0
Do. do.	do.	8 stops, 2 swells & couplers		9	0	0
Do. do.	do.	10 stops, do. do.		10	10	0
Harmonium, very good tone				3	0	0
Do. do.	8 stops ..			5	10	0
Do. do.	12 stops ..			6	0	0

And a great assortment of others.

Please note that the above are **Reliable Musical Instruments**, in first-class condition, and will be exchanged, if desired, any time for a New Instrument.

J. BENTLEY, 42 & 44, High Street
CREWE.

J. Bentley, second-hand seller of pianos and organs. No doubt someone in Crewe still has one of Bentley's fine pianos. The prices certainly make interesting reading!

F. WOOLDRIDGE,

Ironmonger and

CYCLE AGENT

36 & 43, High Street, Crewe.

(SEMI-RACER)

Largest Stock of Cycles in Town

By Discount or Easy Payments.

Call and inspect my display of

TILE REGISTERS, MANTELPIECES,

TILE HEARTHS, KITCHEN RANGES,

&c., &c.

Electric Bells, Gas Fittings, &c.

F. Wooldridge, ironmonger and cycle agent. The only thing that seems to have changed in the last 100 years is the price!

THE REASON WHY

The Working Man should wear only

TAYLOR'S

— SHIRTS.

The following Sales will convince you we
have no equal :—

YEAR.		SALES.	YEAR.		SALES.
1889	...	1550	1894	...	4558
1890	...	1940	1895	...	5320
1891	...	2560	1896	...	5539
1892	...	3314	1897	...	5849
1893	...	3620	1898	...	nearly 1000 more

86, MARKET STREET, CREWE.

Maker-up of the

UNSHRINKABLE MAGNET SHIRTING.

No low-class worthless rubbish kept in stock.

Taylor's Shirts. The confidence shown in the firm's claims suggest that some of the shirts might
still exist today.

WOOLF'S Limited,

South Cheshire Brewery,

WHOLESALE

WINE and SPIRIT DEALERS.

Brewers of the Celebrated

Mild and Bitter Crewe Ales.

FAMILIES SUPPLIED.

EVERY ACCOMMODATION at the

QUEEN'S PARK HOTEL,

ADJOINING.

BILLIARDS.

An Excellent Bowling Green

Is attached, and is absolutely private.

Woolf's Limited, wholesale wine and spirit dealers. The business ran under the name of Edward Samuel Woolf until around 1895. It was situated at the South Cheshire Brewery in Wistaston Road, which adjoined the Queen's Park Hotel. It then became Woolf's Ltd until 1923 when it was taken over by Ind Coope and Co. Ltd. The brewery closed shortly afterwards but it was still listed in 1926, possibly as a depot.

Walter Button, millwright and engineer. While so much of the old Crewe has disappeared above ground, the name of Walter Button still lives on and is seen by thousands of people every week as they pass over cellar covers and grids all around the town.

72

Four
Organizations and Societies

The Western Social and Sports Club (Reg. Office No. 10973 R. Cheshire-affiliated). Members recall playing dominoes in a part of the club with the dubious title of the 'ratpit'. The picture was taken in the mid-1930s by Walton's Studio in Mill Street, Crewe, but does anyone recognize the trophy?

The West Street Baptist Band of Hope, *c.* 1907. The bearded gentleman behind the girl in the sailor suit and big hat was Billy Dawson who lost an arm in a wheel lathe accident in Crewe Works. The young man on the left of Billy Dawson is Frank Kettle. The location of the event is unknown.

Coppenhall Terrace looking towards Chester Bridge. The Commercial Hotel at the top of High Street can be seen in the distance. The scene shows the Boys Life Brigade returning from camp in 1906 amid great jollification. Only three of the gables on the right still exist today and the row of trees has been replaced by a row of shops.

The officers of the West Street Baptist Boys Life Brigade, *c.* 1908. Back row, left to right: Frank Kettle, Reverend T.B. Field, Lt W. Gorrell. Front row: Harry Kettle and C. Goring.

The West Street Baptist Boys Life Brigade at the rear of the old pavilion in Queen's Park, *c.* 1908. The officers along the back of the group are, from left to right: C. Goring, Lt W. Gorrell, Reverend T.B. Field, -?-, Frank Kettle, Harry Kettle. The presence of the stretcher in the foreground would indicate that the boys were trained in some form of first aid.

The 1st Company, Boys Brigade assembled at North Street in Crewe. Back row, left to right: Alan Wells, Norman Wakefield, Frank Dytor, -?-, Jimmy Hough, Fred Wilkinson, Harry Blackburn, Harry Morgan, Harry Whittaker, Ted Taylor, Doug Bailey, Vic Greer, John Sumner, Mick Vickers, Ernie Taylor, Bob Cade, Harry Hughes, -?-. Middle row: Arthur Watson, Arthur Manning, Jimmy Bossons, Reg Clarke, George Ellis, Ivor Timmins, Bill Dunning, Frank Cadman, Fred Phillips, Charlie Moore, Joe Palin, Fred Dean, -?-, Bill Worrall, Cliff Meakin, Howard Bostock, Ken Laycock, Albert Fisher. Front row: -?-, Frank Dudley, -?-, -?-, Ken Bennett, Frank Weston, -?-, Captain Frank Whittaker, Lt Ackroyd, Ernie Lightfoot, -?-, -?-, Dennis Cooper.

The Boys Brigade membership card for 1937-38. The Boys Brigade was formed in 1883 by Sir William A. Smith, the Boys Life Brigade was founded in 1899, and in 1926 the two were united. Boys between the ages of twelve and seventeen could be members.

Members of the St John Ambulance Brigade at the Borough School in 1937. The photograph was taken by Lewis Jones from Mill Street.

Crewe Co-op Band on parade in Market Street in 1957. It is possible to see the old LNWR general offices (extreme left), the Gas Showroom, Martins Dyers and Cleaners with the offices of Road Transport and General Insurance Company Limited above, and Tom Consterdine Ltd, sellers of electrical goods) is next door. No doubt some readers will be able to identify the shop with the blinds. The gables above the shops are relics of old Crewe. The players include: Harold Allcock (trombone), Brian Rushbrooke (bass), Jack Hulme (baritone), Jack Dodd (baritone), Ken Hanks (euphonium), Gordon Tatton (horn), Brenda Ledwards (horn), Glenys Walley (cornet), Norman Williams (cornet), Albert Hillier (cornet), George Wilkinson (cornet), Brian Thornhill (cornet), Arthur Davies (cornet).

Crewe Air Training Corps Band in 1954. On 1 January 1955 it was renamed the Crewe Co-op Band. Back row, left to right: Geoff Hilditch, Arthur Davies, Glenys Walley, Stan ?, Albert Hillier, George Wilkinson, Terry Laycock, Norman Williams, Jack Snelson. Middle row: Jack Hulme, -?-, Jimmy Moston, Harold Allcock, -?-, Gordon Tatton, Albert Birchenough, Jack Dodd. Front row: Harold Dean, Jack Hewitt, Alec Udale, Bass Stokes (musical director), Bill Cooper Snr, Eddie Ash, Brian Rushbrooke.

The Crewe West End Silver Band ready for a brass band contest in Manchester in 1955. What great contests they had in those days at Belle Vue, the showground of the North, with its zoological gardens, funfair featuring the 'Bobs' and the speedway. Unfortunately, all this has now disappeared. The picture, taken off West Street, includes Bob Fletcher the bandmaster on the far right, and his two sons. Others present include: Craig Webb, Geoff Dawson, Alan Newton, Bill Sharratt, Alan Price, Harry Neild, John Davies, Roy Butler, Fred Woods, Wilf Kirkham, Harold Bourne, Dave Morris, George Barker, Hector McGrath, Arthur Mullock.

Amalgamated Engineering Union, Crewe District Committee, in 1934. Back row, left to right: S. Simpson, R. Platt, G. Ellis, W.G. Swallow, R.J. Mansfield, H. Andrews, F.R. Lloyd, Alderman J. Smith JP. Front row: T. Talbot (District Secretary), Alderman F. Bott (District President), J.C. Little (President Executive Council), Councillor C.R. Bates, R. Openshaw.

Florence (Flo) and Tom Bostock behind the bar at the old Sydney Working Men's Club. Flo and Tom were steward and stewardess for almost fourteen years from the late 1930s until the early 1950s. The building was made of corrugated iron but was eventually replaced by the present club. The club was originally founded in a large house next to the chapel in Howard Street. When the First World War was over the committee bought the corrugated iron building and it was erected on the present site. This was heated by a Nelson-type stove with a chimney through the roof. Herbert Richard Davies was one of the founder members. His daughter Elsie and her husband Ernie Perkins were steward and stewardess for many years between the wars. There was a billiard table in the centre of the room but the bar had no pumps as all the beer was kept in barrels on low stillages. Does anyone remember the Forest Brown Ale on sale in the picture?

Many happy events were staged in the old club and this Christmas party from around 1952 was no exception. The little girl with the white socks in the left centre is Pat Hadaway (now Mrs Nott). Also in the picture are Pat's brother Bill, Beryl Perkins (Elsie's daughter), Anne Dewson and Colin Barber. Tom Bostock, the steward, worked hard cultivating produce in his garden to raise funds for these popular events. Sadly the club has recently closed.

Crewe Rolls Royce Fire Brigade competing for the Oldham Trophy at the Works Fire Brigade Contest in 1955. Back row, left to right: Walter Kirkland, George Ford, Bob Dodd, Bill Curzon, Eric Walley. Front row: Ronnie Best, O.V. Valentine, Bill Jones.

Five
Sporting and
General Events

The Mayor of Crewe's Ball in 1936. The Mayor's Ball was once an annual event.

Crewe Carnival procession, c. 1906. It must have been quite an ordeal to walk around the processional route on a pair of stilts as these lads are doing. The shops are, left to right: Strangward and Plumb the baker's, with Hovis bread advertised; G.R. Ball, auction mart, 49 Nantwich Road, with a To Let sign evident; and Philip Platt, ladies' mantles and costumiers.

Many people put considerable effort into the carnival ninety years ago. These floats represent Barnum and Bunkum's Circus. The first carriage carries Mr Barnum and Mr Bunkum, the second Barnum and Bunkum's Silver and Brass Band, and the first of the three cages is labelled Barnum and Bunkum's Gingerbread Lions. The cages, however, contain humans rather than animals! In those days it seemed as if everyone in the crowd wore a hat.

A mysterious troupe of what appear to be Chinese vases taking part in the Crewe Carnival around 1906. Police Constable No. 173 looks on as the troupe stops to have their photograph taken. After hours stuck inside one of these costumes on a boiling hot day, it is remarkable that anybody finished the course. These events brought out tens of thousands of spectators. A painted poster in the background that reads, Cycles Stored Here shows that there was always someone ready to take advantage of the situation. The photograph was taken by J.L. Hart, 52 Nantwich Road.

Another entry in this popular event. The float advertises Millar's Mandolin College and has six players with five bow back mandolins and one banjo-type instrument. The boy on the left has a collecting box. The decorated bicycle is titled A Saxon Prince. The costumes are superb.

Miss Mary Roddan ('Mary and her Little Lamb') at the Victoria Farm, Herbert Street, Sydney. The fête was opened by radio personality Dan Archer.

Washing day at Westminster Street Nursery in 1953. The building is in the playground beside the old bandstand.

SILVER JUBILEE CREWE.
÷ 1935 ÷

A party at Cemetery Road celebrating the Silver Jubilee of King George V and Queen Mary in 1935. What is now Badger Avenue can be seen running across the picture. There appear to be around sixty children and thirty women in the group but only eight male adults. They were probably at work or otherwise engaged in the local hostelry when the picture was taken.

A children's party at Deneside Avenue, Coppenhall, celebrating VE Day.

Peel Street Coronation celebrations in 1953. Note the whitened kerbstones on both sides of the road, bunting, tubs of flowers along the length of the street and not a car in sight.

Coronation celebrations in Hulme Street (off West Street), with Crewe Works in the background. Events like this brought the community together.

A happy gathering during a Catherine Street Coronation party in 1953. This field was at the side of the Frances Street Printing Works (formerly the Express Works).

The residents of Peel Street, Ramsbottom Street and Richard Moon Street enjoy a day excursion to Champion Bakeries in the late 1950s. The ladies can be seen clutching their goody bags. Back row, left to right: Mrs L. Bolivar, Mrs Ivy Hughes, Mrs D. Bryan, -?- (Mrs Bolivar's sister-in-law), Muriel Elsie Walton, Mrs Harry Morris, Margaret ?, Mrs Grosvenor, Mrs M. Harvey, Margaret Welch, Mrs Welch. Front row: Mrs Bryan, Mrs Clewes, Mrs Eye, Mrs Ida Shaw, Mrs Louth, Mrs D. Mason, Mrs Gladys Wall, Mrs Rubbathan, -?-. The trip was arranged by Mrs Gladys Wall, the owner of the grocer's shop on the corner of Peel Street and Richard Moon Street. The shop's entrance was in Peel Street.

Mrs Cooper and her daughter Joyce outside the old Marks and Spencer store in 1934.

Beryl Warwick (née Price) aged ten. She won first prize in the Cheshire Stage Dancing Festival in 1946.

Dancers at Rattigans School of Dancing in Mill Street in 1946. Back row, left to right: Beryl Price, Joan Williams, Joan Lindop, Jean Clark who became Crewe Mayoress when she was Mrs Salmon. Front row: Jean Lithgoe, ? Simpson, Shirley Mitchell.

The opening of Willsons fashion shop on Friday 12 May 1957. Hundreds gathered to witness the arrival of the Mayor and Mayoress, Mr and Mrs G.E. Hodgkinson, and the singer Miss Carole Carr, before they performed the ceremony.

The Mayor and Mayoress escort Miss Carole Carr around Willsons' new store. Although it may not appear so, this must have been one of the Mayor's more pleasant engagements.

The reopening of Crewe Theatre by the famous radio comedian Jack Train, around 1956. He is signing the visitors book in the Municipal Buildings in the presence of Mr Alan Brook, the Town Clerk, and the Mayor and Mayoress.

The Civic Procession on 27 May 1956 passes Market Square on its way to Trinity Church in Mill Street; a Wesleyan Methodist church with 1,000 seats. The procession is led by the Mayor's attendant carrying the Civic Mace followed by Mayor G.E. Hodgkinson, the Town Clerk and the Mayoress dressed in a white coat. The Mayor's attendant is just passing the W.H. Smith shop. Although there was no bus station at this time, some buses started and terminated around the square. Crosville Motor Services' shop and office were conveniently located here. The shop advertised their outings and parcel services as well as selling sweets and tobacco. A bus timetable was on offer at the cost of sixpence. Many readers will remember W. Smallwood's shop, particularly a later one further down Market Street, which always had a good supply of fish, game, poultry and rabbits hanging outside.

Crewe Alexandra supporters queuing for tickets in 1960 when 'The Alex' were drawn against the mighty Tottenham Hotspur. The game at Gresty Road was watched by almost 20,000 supporters, substantially more than the modern full house of less than 6,000. The Alex held Spurs to a 2-2 draw on the day but went down by the astonishing score of 13-2 in the replay. Can you find yourself in the photograph?

Alan Geldard, who represented Great Britain in the 1948 Olympics at Herne Hill, showing his paces at the Crewe Goddard Street Sports Meeting in August 1948.

The Norton motorcycle on which A.J. Bell won the Senior Tourist Trophy in 1948. The display was in the Crewe Town Hall on the night of the Crewe and South Cheshire Ball.

Crewe Works' welding shop, *c.* 1950. Back row, left to right: F. Pugh, -?-, J. Hall, D. Beswick, J. Roberts, J. Dutton, H. Whalley, T. Bache, L. Davis, T. Taylor. Front row: H. Owen, E. Heath, C. Ogden, B. Jones, I.C. Forsyth (Works Manager), A. Large, H. Rowlands, -?-, S. Dutton.

Crewe Works' welding shop, *c.* 1950. Back row, left to right: C. Griffiths, H. Vickers, F. Trickett, J. Podmore, S. Dutton, J. Hall, J. Roberts, J. Dutton, H. Whalley, L. Davis, Mr Brown (Assistant Manager), T. Taylor, J. Lowndes, -?-. Middle row: J. Wakefield, B. Jones, I.C. Forsyth (Works Manager), T. Bache, A. Large. Front: C. Ogden, D. Beswick, H. Rowlands.

A bowls presentation in front of the pavilion at the Earl of Crewe in the 1920s. Harry Jennings is second from the left on the front row and sixth left is Billy White, the Mayor of Crewe at one time.

Harry Jennings (left) was a fine bowler and is seen here on the green at the Earl of Crewe before the First World War. The impressive castellated terrace in the background is Sherwin Street.

The LMR Sports Club Dramatic Society's presentation of Esther McCracken's *No Medals* was given on 27 October 1948 at Crewe Works canteen in Goddard Street. The cast for this production were: Peter Grahl, Dilys Edwards, Wilf Edwards, Renee Bradshaw, Jimmy Flood, Hilda Moses, Margaret Jolly, Elizabeth Dudley, Helen Wyland, Frank Low, Eric Johnson, Leonard Fleet, Irene Elks, Marion Rutherford, Edward Makin.

Popular local performer Georgie Beck was a great Old Mother Riley impersonator. In the mid-1950s he went to work with Kitty McShane as a stand-in for Arthur Lucan, but after a short while George found he could not work with McShane and returned to do the twelve week summer season of Music Hall at the Crewe Theatre. George lived in Capesthorne Road.

Six

Education

Mr Kilby at Crewe Grammar School, Ruskin Road, in 1948. This recreates the atmosphere of a maths lesson from half a century ago.

The London and North Western Railway built Bedford Street School in the early 1900s. This fine building was demolished during March 1999 to make way for housing development.

Bedford Street School's U14 medal-winning team from 1912. The lads' medals are hooked onto the shield. Little did they know that in five or six years some of them would be fighting for their country in the First World War.

The girls class at Borough School (more recently Brierley Street School), *c.* 1910. The class appears to have around thirty-six pupils who are well-dressed and sitting with hands behind backs.

St Mary's infants in 1928. Back row, second left is Eddie Heaps, third left is William Evans and extreme right is Walter Harding. Middle row, fifth left is Margaret Bennett. Front row, extreme left is Clare Wyatt, second left is Kath Emmett and third left is Betty Murphy.

County Secondary School, Crewe, in 1923. Back row, left to right: -?-, Kathleen Sylvester, Nancy Meeres, Margaret Hitchen, -?-, Evelyn Morris, Doris Leech. Front row: Enid Tipping, Lucy Collins, Margery Dodd, Muriel Reay, Hilda Edwards, Miss Fidler (teacher), Nancy Edwards, -?-, ? Edwards, Olive Metcalfe, Sybil Ellis.

The children of Hightown Infants in 1925 were asked to bring their toys to school. The young girl in the middle of the centre row, holding a black teddy bear, is Joan Cottrell, now Mrs Joan Doig. There is also a spinning top, an elephant, a concertina, numerous teddies and dolls, and the lad on the right would feel particularly proud to be the owner of such a fine motor car.

Pupils of Mill Street Junior School in 1934. This photograph is not of a class but a group of brothers and sisters who attended the school at the same time. Fred Harding is in the centre of the back row with his brother Harold on his right. To his left are Jack and Bob Egerton. In front of the Hardings are Arthur (left) and Eric Wickham, whose parents were hosts of the nearby Globe Inn. On the extreme left of the second and thirds rows are the Coopers (brother and sister) whose parents kept a paper shop in Mill Street. Next to them are the Evans', also brother and sister. On the extreme right, sitting on the bench, is Eric Wrench. Sitting on Eric's right is Bernard Ganner and behind is his brother George. In the middle of the seated bench, with dark hair and white dresses, are the Butler sisters who lived in Bank Street and reclining left and right on the carpet are the Hill twins, daughter of haulage contractor Gordon Hill. Between them is one of the Bratt sisters, also of Bank Street, with the other behind her, sitting to the left.

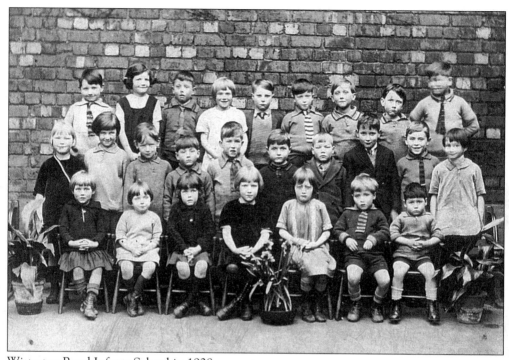

Wistaston Road Infants School in 1928.

The babies class at Borough School, *c.* 1930.

Borough School, now Brierley Street School, c. 1930. The top class teacher was Miss Cornes.

The eight-year-old pupils of Wistaston Road Infants School, c. 1947. Back row, left to right: Phyllis Baxter, -?-, -?-, Jean Slack, John Davenport, Betty Burrows, Ivan ?, Beryl Smith, Colin Sandland, Janet Walker, Dorothy Henshall. Middle row: -?-, Sheila Birch, Ian Hancock, Glenys Walley, Keith ?, Janet Bennion, John Coupe, -?-, Sylvia Harrison, Robert Banks, Margaret Hartley, Alan Butt. Front row: Colin ?, -?-, Maureen Cox, ? Edge, Pamela Mountford, John Bayliss, Sheila Riley, Neville Jones, Margaret White, Ian Twiss, Peter Morris.

Edleston Road School, *c.* 1940. Back row, extreme left is Brian Challinor, second left is Petronela Leeson and fourth left is Peter Young. Front row, second left is Brian Chesworth and second right is Barry Barker.

West Street Junior Mixed School 1947-48. Back row, left to right: Mr Stubbs, Ron Clarke, Terry Kettle, Malcolm Capper, Roy Sproston, Brian Clarkson, Ken Bennett. Front row: Maurice Jenks, Brian Dodd, John Bennion, Terry Dawes, John Dobson. The school has since been converted into the Adtranz works canteen but there is a strong possibility that it may be demolished to make way for a new road in the not too distant future.

The Ludford Street team were 2nd Division winners of the Schools Senior Football League in the 1951-52 season, ending it with a record of played twelve, won ten, drawn one and lost one. They scored forty-four goals and conceded eighteen. Back row: Mr Quine (headmaster), T. Sleigh, A. Barton, B. Charlesworth, H. Williams (teacher), G. Downing, D. Lowndes, H. Lea (teacher). Middle row: K. Kirby, K. Podmore, C.J. Metcalf, R. Foster, D. Murray. Front row: K. Bennett, R. Meakin. Robin Smith also played but is missing from the photograph.

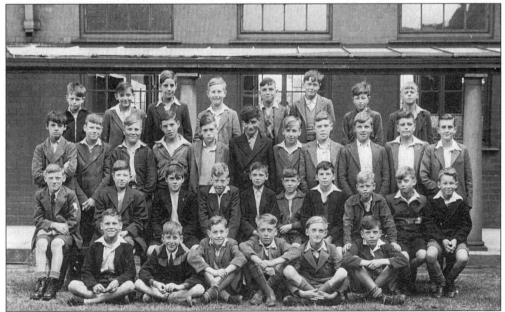

A boys class at Ludford Street Day School in 1950.

The Shavington Council School football team in the 1951-52 season. Back row, left to right: Lou Barnett (headmaster), Ray Parker, Ray Dale, Fred Cope, David Wilson, David Keen, Mr Tom Steventon (master). Middle row: Alan ?, -?-, Alan Newton, Phillip Elson, ? Dawson. Front right is Charlie Young. Alan Newton, who captained the team, is well known today as a popular trombonist in the local band, Salt City Jazzmen, and a ukulele enthusiast in the South Cheshire George Formby Society.

Crewe County Grammar were Schools' Road Safety Quiz champions in 1953. Back row: Glenys Walley, Olive Steele, Mary Eckersley, Sheila Goldsmith. Front row: Janice Brookshaw, Barbara Wood, Margaret Hartley, Sylvia Harrison.

Seven

Haslington

The Victoria Laundry, Haslington, in 1912. The firm's transport at the time was by means of a horse-drawn vehicle, an early motor van and a bicycle. The manageress at the time was Miss Gollefor who claimed that the nearest way to a healthy and happy home was via her laundry as it made the household linen pure and sweet. The firm, who also performed dry cleaning, had a van that made collections within a radius of twenty miles.

The Main Road looking in the direction of Crewe around 1920. The sign on the post indicates that there was a public telephone in the house. No doubt the driver of the motorcycle combination M6720 on the front and MEJ 20 on the back is making a telephone call. A coalman and his horse and cart drive up the centre of the road and the church tower peeps over the tops of the houses in the middle of the picture.

Main Road, Haslington, at Fox's corner. The house on the left has since been demolished.

Main Road, Haslington, looking towards the corner of Mere Street. T.R. Mould's, the grocers and bakers shop on the left, is decorated with enamel signs advertising Fry's Chocolate, Fry's Cocoa, Brooke Bonds Tea, Coleman's Starch and Mustard, Mackintosh's Toffee, Hudson's Soap and, in the window, bills advertising Crewe Cinemas.

There was once a mere by Main Road in Haslington. This was situated roughly on the site of the Pinfold Nurseries and where Eton Hall Nursing Home stands today. As a main road, this says little for the state of side roads in those days.

A view looking back towards Mould's shop showing the mere and village in flood. The road has disappeared completely.

Looking towards Crewe, with the position of the road indicated by the storm lamps hanging from metal stakes.

Haslington Hall dates from around 1480 and was once the home of Admiral Sir John Vernon. Some of the beams in the house are said to be from ships which engaged the Spanish Armada.

The Hawk Inn complete with thatch on a warm summer's day in the 1920s. An AA sign can be seen underneath the porch and the metal sign advertises Jones' Sewing Machines. The house on the right has a sign in the window advertising Mrs Newton the dressmaker.

The Hawk Inn in the 1920s, looking towards Sandbach. The ubiquitous highwayman Dick Turpin is said to have stabled his horse here.

Haslington Parish War Memorial reads, 'To the Glory of God and in loving memory of the following men who gave their lives in the Great War 1914-1918'. A smaller tablet has been added for those who were killed in the Second World War. Twenty-four local boys gave their lives in the First World War and seven in the Second World War.

The interior of St Matthew's Church, Haslington. Note the lighting is by oil lamp and the number of floral decorations.

Stonemasons at work in Haslington in the 1920s. Note the celluloid collars. Does any reader recognize the site?

This pump and stone trough was once a feature of Haslington. Does anyone know if it still exists?

Eight

Wistaston

A rare view of Wistaston Mill around the time of the First World War. The fields in the distance have now been fully developed into housing estates.

Brigadier-General Walthall, DSO of Wistaston Hall.

Wistaston Primary School, showing Mr Hutton the headmaster with his class. Back row, fourth left is Jim Holland

Wistaston School, around 1920, with headmaster Mr Hutton on the left. Middle row, second right is Mary Holland, aged thirteen.

Wistaston School, *c.* 1927. The teacher is Miss Evanson and the headmaster at the time was Mr Platt.

Wistaston Church in 1955, prior to the building of the church hall. It would appear that there were greenhouses on the site, which probably belonged to James' Nurseries.

The front view of Whitegates farmhouse on Wistaston Green Road in the 1930s. Like most small farms and large smallholdings of the era, the most important function of Whitegates was to allow the farmer and his family to be self-sufficient, with enough left over to sell in the local markets to raise additional cash. The farm had a small dairy herd for the sale of milk on a daily basis as well as hens, geese, turkeys and pigs.

Whitegates Farm, a large smallholding on Wistaston Green Road, c. 1955. The farm, which was part of the Walthall Estate, was bought by Mr Woodcock, a local farmer and butcher, and was rented to the Holland family. Their tenancy came to an end when Nantwich Rural Council invoked a Compulsory Purchase Order on the land in order to build a council estate. The farm was located on the left of Wistaston Green Road, opposite the entrance of Handforth Road, on what is now Whitegates Council Estate.

Haymaking at Whitegates Farm, *c.* 1930.

Hay-time at Whitegates Farm. A scene no
longer part of rural life.

Beryl Warwick with a sheepdog. Beryl's father Jack Price set up home in Wistaston Green Road and worked at Whitegates Farm, along with his brother-in-law George Ernest Holland.

Beryl Warwick with a pet lamb at Whitegates Farm.

The construction of the sewage works off Wistaston Green Road, between the wars. George Ernest Holland, farmer of Whitegates Farm, was the superintendent of the sewage works for many years.

Filter beds at the Wistaston Sewage Works after completion. After closure, the works lay desolate for a number of years and became a source of danger for local youngsters who were fascinated by the place. The site was eventually cleared around 1990 and the area is now a popular walk from Wistaston Green Road to the bottom of the Hall Bank.

Jim Holland (left) a local joiner, undertaker and farrier, and Jack Price a local farmer on parade in the Home Guard in 1942. The picture was taken at Whitegates Farm.

The staff of the Ministry of Agriculture, Fisheries and Food at Berkeley Towers, Wistaston, in 1948. The building dates from 1892 and was the home of Alfred Silvester Day. His initials can be seen between the third set of windows from the left. Mr Day continued in his father's footsteps in the family business which was founded in the mid-nineteenth century and gained international prominence in the field of animal medicine. Mr Day lived in the house until his death in 1905. His widow married Mr W.H.M. Briant who lived there until 1921, when Mr Harry Willcock, a local businessman, purchased the house. On the demise of Mr Willcock in 1942, the house was bought by Mr William Yoxall, a local builder, who leased it out. The Ministry of Works became owners in 1972.

A special event at the Wistaston Memorial Hall, *c.* 1953. Among those in the picture are: Mr Armitage, Ted Holland, Stan Davies (with hat), Mr Probutt, Jean Owen, Mr Holmes, Mr Latham, Lew Evans, Tom Brown, Mrs Young, Mrs Edge, Mrs Oaks, Mrs Bell, Mrs Ainsell, Mrs Holmes, Vie Buckley, Doris Davies, Mrs Birtles, Mrs Brown, Gladys Edwards, Mrs Sykes, Mr Timmis, Mrs Hodgkisson, Mrs Timmis and Annie Holland.

Mrs Hodgkisson cuts a birthday cake in the Memorial Hall. Mrs Holmes is centre right and Mr Wycherley is the gentleman with the bow tie. The event was probably a celebration for the tenth anniversary of the hall opening.

Sergeant Duffy, the Wistaston bobby, *c.* 1940.